Bunny Pancakes
for Nino and Ari

Story by Isha Lerner

Pictures by Vicki Fredricks

Power of Flower Publishing
Copyright 2021

For Nino and Ari,

Love Nana

In the early morning light,
Mama and the twins are awake.

Shhhh Mama says...

We don't want to wake up Frankie...
asleep in her room.

Shhhh Mama says...

We don't want to wake up Dada...
warm in his bed.

And, we don't want to wake up Henry
...not just yet.

In the kitchen, it's breakfast time.

Mama makes pancakes in the shape of little bunnies.

Once they are cooked just right,
Mama puts yummy bunny pancakes
on shiny blue plates.

She pours warm maple syrup all over
the bunny pancake's ears.

While Frankie sleeps,
and Dada dreams in his warm cozy bed...

The early morning sun
begins to shine through the window.

Another happy day
for Nino and Ari has begun.

Made in the USA
Coppell, TX
05 December 2021